Going Places Maths

About Starters Maths books

STARTERS MATHS have been designed to highlight for young children some everyday situations, to which New Mathematics apply. The topic approach has been used to help the children relate mathematics to the ordinary world around them, by presenting money, number, shape, size and other mathematical ideas in familiar contexts. Children will be able to consolidate their experience in arranging sets, in recognising simple geometric forms and in using other mathematical ideas in ways now widely practised by their teachers. The books also follow the normal school practice of using only metric measures.

The text of each book is simple enough to enable children to read the questions for themselves, as the vocabulary has been carefully controlled to ensure that about 90% of the words used will be familiar to them.

Illustrated by: Geoff Hocking

Written and planned by: Leslie Foster, former Primary School Headmaster and Inspector for Schools, author of *Colour Factor in Action, Play's the Thing, Classes and Counts, Countdown to Christmas, Countdown to Easter* and *Just Look At Computers*.

Managing editor: Su Swallow

Editors: Sandie Oram, Diana Finley

Production: Rosemary Bishop

Chairman, teacher panel: F. F. Blackwell, former General Inspector for Schools, London Borough of Croydon, with responsibility for Primary Education.

Teacher panel: Ruth Lucas, Linda Snowden, Mary Todd

ISBN 0 356 04645 1
(cased edition)

ISBN 0 356 11104 0
(limp edition)

© Macdonald and Company (Publishers) Limited 1974
Reprinted 1984
Made and printed in Great Britain by Hazell, Watson & Viney Limited
Aylesbury, Buckinghamshire

First published in 1974 by Macdonald and Company (Publishers) Limited
Maxwell House
Worship Street
London EC2A 2EN

Members of BPCC plc

STARTERS
MATHS

Going Places
Maths

Macdonald Educational

All these people are going somewhere.
How many are going a long way?
How many are in the set going by air?

2

People travel in different ways.
The astronaut travels in a spaceship.
Can you match a person
to each kind of transport?

3

What can you say about this set?
How many members are in the picture?
Does an aeroplane belong to this set?

4

Can you sort these into two sets?
How many travel on water?
How many fly in the air?
How many more has the sailing set?

There are buildings everywhere.
Look at the tall and the low buildings.
Can you see the shapes they make?

These buildings are in different countries.
Some buildings are symmetrical.
One side balances the other.
Are all these buildings symmetrical?

BUS STOP

This village has a church.
The bus stop is one kilometre away.
What place is one kilometre
from your home?
8

BUS STOP

Here is a map of the village.
Find the church and the bus stop.
How long does it take you to walk
one kilometre from your house?

Here are some wheels
from long ago.
You can see how wheels
have changed.

10

Wheels help things to move easily.
When wheels turn we say they rotate.
One whole turn of a wheel
is called a revolution.

next coach for
LEEDS
leaves at 09.00

This coach holds 29 passengers.
How many seats will be empty?
When does the coach leave?
12

Arrivals		Departures	
Paris	09.00	Milan	09.30
Brussels	09.20	Paris	09.45
Rome	09.40	Bonn	10.00

08 45

luggage
allowance
20kg per person

These people are arriving at the airport.
A machine weighs their luggage.
What takes the luggage to the plane?

13

100 of these
are worth
1 of this

Each country has its own money.
Most countries use decimal currency.
One hundred pennies are worth
one pound.

14

The family are on holiday.
Father photographs the dog.
The picture can be made bigger.
The shape of the dog stays the same.

15

Mosaics are found in many countries.
Can you see the patterns they make?

16

Mosaics are made from tiny pieces
of stone.
Sometimes glass or marble is used.
Can you make mosaic pictures?

How many people will each car hold?
Which of these holds most people?
Arrange them in order of how many
they hold.

18

These crafts go at different speeds.
Which one goes very fast?
Which is slowest of all?

It is busy on the motorway.
Look at the junction.
Find the way along the roads
with your finger.

There are many signs on the roads.
They have shapes on them.
What do the shapes tell us?
What do these road signs mean?

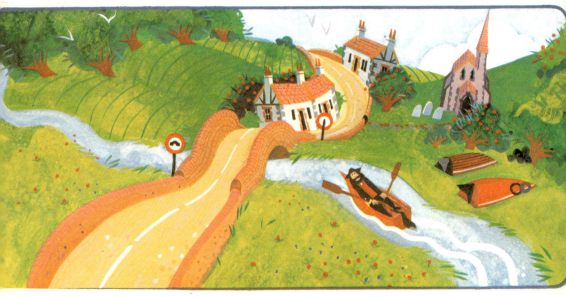

In some countries it is very hot.
In others it is very cold.
How do we measure the temperature?

The time is different
at different places around the world.
We can measure time on a clock.
Can you make a clock to measure time?

23

Look at these vehicles.
Some are longer than others.
Which is longest of all?
Which two are the same length?

24

The white strip is 1 unit long.
How long are the others?
Which is the longest?
How many are shorter than the red one?

Can you count these groups of people :
What numeral goes in these boxes?

5,2 ⟶ ☐   3,6 ⟶ ☐   1,4 ⟶ ☐

26

Falling water makes lovely shapes
and patterns.
It is very strong, and has great force.

Index

Notes for Parents and Teachers

Here is a brief explanation of the various mathematical points covered in this book; to help the interested adult to explore the topic with children.

Sets and numbers *(pages 2, 3, 4, 5, 12, 14, 18, 26)*

Sets are the starting point in modern mathematics. Children sort things into sets and put them in order by size, colour or type *(2, 4, 5, 18)*. They learn to count by matching an object in one set to a thing or person in another set *(3, 4, 5, 26)*. Through various counting exercises with sets, they develop an understanding of the process involved in addition and subtraction *(12, 26)* and the handling of decimal currency *(14)*.

Quantity *(pages 2, 6, 8, 9, 12, 13, 19, 22, 23, 24, 25)*

Children learn the general terms used in mathematical comparisons *(6, 8, 10, 12, 13, 19, 22, 23, 24)* and the more specific terms concerning distance and linear measure *(2, 8, 9, 25)*. They are helped with their ideas about time and speed *(9, 19, 23)* and the measurement of temperature *(22)*.

Space *(pages 6, 7, 10, 11, 15, 16, 17, 20, 21, 27)*

Children learn about simple geometric shapes and patterns *(6, 16, 17, 21, 27)*. They begin to understand the meaning of ideas about movements such as rotation and revolution helped by practical examples *(10, 11)*. Symmetry and enlargement are used to help them understand more about shape *(7, 15)* and they are introduced to the idea of networks *(20)* which is important in work later on topology.

Mechanisms *(pages 13, 27)*

Science and mathematics are closely linked studies. Simple mechanisms which illustrate things like force are now included in most maths courses.